MW01051182

Hooded Scarves
Book 2

Fast to crochet, these hooded scarves make wonderful fashion accessories. Choose a look that complements your personality, or make several so you can always match your mood, whether you're feeling sweet, sassy, or sophisticated. They're great for gifts, too!

LEISURE ARTS, INC. • Maumelle, Arkansas

EMMA

 **EASY**

Finished Scarf Measurement:

8" x 72¼" (20.5 cm x 183.5 cm) (excluding fringe)

Finished Hood Size:

One size fits most Adults

SHOPPING LIST

Yarn (Medium Weight)

[7 ounces, 370 yards (198 grams, 338 meters) per skein]:

☐ Berry - 2 skeins

☐ Grey - 1 skein

Crochet Hook

☐ Size I (5.5 mm) **or** size needed for gauge

GAUGE INFORMATION

In pattern, 2 repeats = 3" (7.5 cm); 4 rows = 2¼" (5.75 cm)

Gauge Swatch: 4½" (11.5 cm) square

With Berry, ch 19.

Rows 1-8: Work same as Scarf, page 4: 11 sts and 4 sps.

—— STITCH GUIDE ——

📹 **FRONT POST SINGLE CROCHET**
(abbreviated FPsc)

Insert hook from **front** to **back** around post of st indicated *(Fig. 4, page 31)*, YO and pull up a loop (2 loops on hook), YO and draw through both loops on hook.

INSTRUCTIONS
SCARF

When joining yarn and finishing off, leave a 7" (18 cm) length to be worked into fringe.

With Berry, ch 244, place marker in fourth ch from hook for Edging placement.

Row 1 (Right side): Dc in fourth ch from hook (**3 skipped chs count as first dc**) and in next ch, skip next 2 chs, dc in next ch, ★ 3 dc in next ch, dc in next ch, skip next 2 chs, dc in next ch; repeat from ★ across to last ch, 2 dc in last ch; finish off: 241 dc.

Note: Loop a short piece of yarn around any stitch to mark Row 1 as **right** side.

Row 2: With **wrong** side facing, 📹 join Grey with sc in first dc *(see Joining With Sc, page 31)*; sc in next dc, ★ ch 3, skip next 2 dc, sc in next dc, work FPsc around next dc, sc in next dc; repeat from ★ across to last 4 dc, ch 3, skip next 2 dc, sc in last 2 dc; finish off: 145 sts and 48 ch-3 sps.

Row 3: With **right** side facing, 📹 join Berry with dc in first sc *(see Joining With Dc, page 31)*; 5 dc in next ch-3 sp and in each ch-3 sp across to last 2 sc, skip next sc, dc in last sc; finish off: 242 dc.

Row 4: With **wrong** side facing, join Grey with sc in first dc; ch 1, skip next dc, sc in next dc, work FPsc around next dc, sc in next dc, ★ ch 3, skip next 2 dc, sc in next dc, work FPsc around next dc, sc in next dc; repeat from ★ across to last 2 dc, ch 1, skip next dc, sc in last dc; finish off: 146 sts and 49 sps.

Row 5: With **right** side facing, join Berry with dc in first sc; 2 dc in same st, skip next ch-1 sp, 5 dc in next ch-3 sp and in each ch-3 sp across to last ch-1 sp, skip next ch-1 sp, 3 dc in last sc; finish off: 241 dc.

Rows 6-14: Repeat Rows 2-5 twice, then repeat Row 2 once **more**: 145 sts and 48 ch-3 sps.

HOOD

Row 1: With **right** side of Scarf facing, skip first 18 ch-3 sps and next sc, join Berry with dc in next FPsc; 5 dc in each of next 12 ch-3 sps, skip next sc, dc in next FPsc, leave remaining 18 ch-3 sps unworked; finish off: 62 dc.

Row 2: With **wrong** side facing, join Grey with sc in first dc; ch 1, skip next dc, sc in next dc, work FPsc around next dc, sc in next dc, ★ ch 3, skip next 2 dc, sc in next dc, work FPsc around next dc, sc in next dc; repeat from ★ across to last 2 dc, ch 1, skip next dc, sc in last dc; finish off: 38 sts and 13 sps.

Row 3: With **right** side facing, join Berry with dc in first sc; 2 dc in same st, skip next ch-1 sp, 5 dc in next ch-3 sp and in each ch-3 sp across to last ch-1 sp, skip last ch-1 sp, 3 dc in last sc; finish off: 61 dc.

Row 4: With **wrong** side facing, join Grey with sc in first dc; sc in next dc, ★ ch 3, skip next 2 dc, sc in next dc, work FPsc around next dc, sc in next dc; repeat from ★ across to last 4 dc, ch 3, skip next 2 dc, sc in last 2 dc; finish off: 37 sts and 12 ch-3 sps.

Row 5: With **right** side facing, join Berry with dc in first sc; 5 dc in next ch-3 sp and in each ch-3 sp across to last 2 sc, skip next sc, dc in last sc; finish off: 62 dc.

Rows 6-9: Repeat Rows 2-5; at end of Row 9, do **not** finish off.

Joining Row (Back Hood seam)**:** Ch 1, turn; 🎥 fold Hood in half with **right** side together; matching sts on Row 9 and working through **outside** loops of **both** thicknesses, sc in each st across; finish off.

TRIM

With **right** side of Hood facing, join Berry with sc in end of Row 1; 🎥 sc evenly across end of rows; finish off.

EDGING

With **wrong** side facing, 🎥 working in free loops of beginning ch *(Fig. 3, page 31)*, join Grey with sc in marked ch; sc in next ch, ★ ch 3, skip next 2 chs, sc in next ch, work FPsc around same dc on Row 1 as previous FPsc, sc in next ch; repeat from ★ across to last 4 chs, ch 3, skip next 2 chs, sc in last 2 chs; finish off: 145 sts and 48 ch-3 sps.

FRINGE

Add additional fringe across short edges of Scarf as follows:
Cut a piece of cardboard 3" (7.5 cm) wide and 8" (20.5 cm) long. Wind corresponding color yarn **loosely** and **evenly** lengthwise around the cardboard until the card is filled, then cut across one end; repeat as needed.

Hold 3 strands of corresponding color yarn and fold in half.

🎥 With **wrong** side facing and using a crochet hook, draw the folded end up through a row and pull the loose ends through the folded end *(Fig. 1a)*; draw the knot up **tightly** *(Fig. 1b)*. Repeat across each short edge. Lay Scarf flat on a hard surface and trim the ends.

Fig. 1a

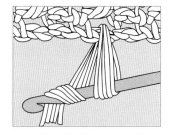

Fig. 1b

Design by Lois J. Long.

LISA

 **EASY**

Finished Scarf Measurement:

7½" x 74" (19 cm x 188 cm)

Finished Hood Size:

One size fits most Adults

SHOPPING LIST

Yarn (Medium Weight)
[6 ounces, 315 yards (170 grams, 288 meters) per skein]:

☐ 3 skeins

Crochet Hook

☐ Size H (5 mm) **or** size needed for gauge

GAUGE INFORMATION

In pattern, 3 repeats = 4¾" (12 cm);

12 rows = 5" (12.75 cm)

Gauge Swatch: 5" (12.75 cm) square

Ch 20.

Rows 1-12: Work same as Scarf, page 8: 13 sts and
12 ch-1 sps.

Finish off.

STITCH GUIDE

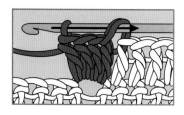 POPCORN (uses one sc)

4 Dc in sc indicated, drop loop from hook, insert hook in first dc of 4-dc group, hook dropped loop and draw through st *(Fig. 2)*, ch 1 to close.

Fig. 2

INSTRUCTIONS
SCARF

Ch 278.

Row 1 (Right side): Sc in second ch from hook and in each ch across: 277 sc.

Note: Loop a short piece of yarn around any stitch to mark Row 1 as **right** side.

Row 2: Ch 1, turn; sc in first sc, ★ ch 1, skip next 2 sc, (dc, ch 1) 3 times in next sc, skip next 2 sc, sc in next sc; repeat from ★ across: 185 sts and 184 ch-1 sps.

Row 3: Ch 6 (**counts as first dc plus ch 3, now and throughout**), turn; skip next dc, sc in next dc, ★ ch 3, skip next dc, work Popcorn in next sc, ch 3, skip next dc, sc in next dc; repeat from ★ across to last dc, ch 3, skip last dc, dc in last sc: 45 Popcorns and 92 ch-3 sps.

Row 4: Ch 1, turn; sc in first dc, ch 1, (dc, ch 1) 3 times in next sc, ★ sc in next Popcorn, ch 1, (dc, ch 1) 3 times in next sc; repeat from ★ across to last dc, sc in last dc: 185 sts and 184 ch-1 sps.

Rows 5-16: Repeat Rows 3 and 4, 6 times: 185 sts and 184 ch-1 sps.

Finish off.

HOOD

Row 1: With **right** side of Scarf facing, skip first 17 3-dc groups and  join yarn with dc in next sc *(see Joining With Dc, page 31)*; ch 3, skip next dc, sc in next dc, ★ ch 3, skip next dc, work Popcorn in next sc, ch 3, skip next dc, sc in next dc; repeat from ★ 10 times **more**, ch 3, skip next dc, dc in next sc, leave remaining 17 3-dc groups unworked: 11 Popcorns and 24 ch-3 sps.

Row 2: Ch 1, turn; sc in first dc, ch 1, (dc, ch 1) 3 times in next sc, ★ sc in next Popcorn, ch 1, (dc, ch 1) 3 times in next sc; repeat from ★ across to last dc, sc in last dc: 49 sts and 48 ch-1 sps.

Row 3: Ch 6, turn; skip next dc, sc in next dc, ★ ch 3, skip next dc, work Popcorn in next sc, ch 3, skip next dc, sc in next dc; repeat from ★ across to last dc, ch 3, skip last dc, dc in last sc: 11 Popcorns and 24 ch-3 sps.

Rows 4-11: Repeat Rows 2 and 3, 4 times: 11 Popcorns and 24 ch-3 sps.

Joining Row (Back Hood seam)**:** Ch 1, turn; fold Hood in half with **right** side together; matching sts on Row 11 and working through **outside** loops of **both** thicknesses, sc in each st across; finish off.

EDGING

Rnd 1: With **right** side of Scarf facing, join yarn with sc *(see Joining With Sc, page 31)* in free loop of first ch *(Fig. 3, page 31)*; sc evenly around **entire** piece working 3 sc in each corner; join with slip st to first sc.

Rnd 2: Ch 1; working from **left** to **right**, work reverse sc in next sc *(Figs. 5a-d, page 31)* and in each sc around; join with slip st to first st, finish off.

Design by Lois J. Long.

9

CHERIE

 **EASY**

Finished Scarf Measurement:

6¾" x 73¾" (17 cm x 187.5 cm)

Finished Hood Size:

One size fits most Adults

SHOPPING LIST

Yarn (Medium Weight)

[7 ounces, 370 yards

(198 grams, 338 meters) per skein]:

☐ 2 skeins

Crochet Hook

☐ Size I (5.5 mm) **or** size needed for gauge

GAUGE INFORMATION

In pattern, 4 repeats and 8 rows = 3½" (9 cm)

Gauge Swatch: 4" x 3½" (10 cm x 9 cm)

Ch 15.

Rows 1-8: Work same as Scarf: 10 dc and

4 ch-1 sps.

Finish off.

INSTRUCTIONS
SCARF
Ch 252.

Row 1: Sc in second ch from hook, ch 1, skip next ch, sc in next ch, ★ ch 3, skip next 2 chs, sc in next ch; repeat from ★ across to last 2 chs, ch 1, skip next ch, sc in last ch: 85 sc and 84 sps.

Row 2 (Right side): Ch 3 **(counts as first dc, now and throughout)**, turn; (dc, ch 1, dc) in next sc and in each sc across to last sc, dc in last sc: 168 dc and 83 ch-1 sps.

Note: Loop a short piece of yarn around any stitch to mark Row 2 as **right** side.

Row 3: Ch 1, turn; sc in first dc, ch 1, sc in next ch-1 sp, (ch 3, sc in next ch-1 sp) across to last 2 dc, ch 1, skip next dc, sc in last dc: 85 sc and 84 sps.

Row 4: Ch 3, turn; (dc, ch 1, dc) in next sc and in each sc across to last sc, dc in last sc: 168 dc and 83 ch-1 sps.

Rows 5-14: Repeat Rows 3 and 4, 5 times: 168 dc and 83 ch-1 sps.

Finish off.

HOOD
Row 1: With **wrong** side of Scarf facing, skip first 30 ch-1 sps and 🎥 join yarn with sc in next dc *(see Joining With Sc, page 31)*; ch 1, sc in next ch-1 sp, (ch 3, sc in next ch-1 sp) 22 times, ch 1, skip next dc, sc in next dc, leave remaining 30 ch-1 sps unworked: 25 sc and 24 sps.

Row 2: Ch 3, turn; (dc, ch 1, dc) in next sc and in each sc across to last sc, dc in last sc: 50 dc and 23 ch-1 sps.

Row 3: Ch 1, turn; sc in first dc, ch 1, sc in next ch-1 sp, (ch 3, sc in next ch-1 sp) across to last 2 dc, ch 1, skip next dc, sc in last dc: 25 sc and 24 sps.

Rows 4-10: Repeat Rows 2 and 3, 3 times; then repeat Row 2 once **more**: 50 dc and 23 ch-1 sps.

Joining Row (Back Hood seam)**:** Ch 1, turn; 🎥 fold Hood in half with **right** side together; matching sts on Row 10 and working through **outside** loops of **both** thicknesses, sc in each st across; finish off.

EDGING
Rnd 1: With **right** side of Scarf facing, join yarn with sc in 🎥 free loop of ch at base of first sc *(Fig. 3, page 31)*; 🎥 sc evenly around entire piece working 3 sc in each corner; join with slip st to first sc, finish off.

Design by Lois J. Long.

ANGELINA

 **EASY**

Finished Scarf Measurement:

6" x 74" (15 cm x 188 cm)

Finished Hood Size:

One size fits most Adults

SHOPPING LIST

Yarn (Bulky Weight)

[6 ounces, 185 yards (170 grams, 169 meters) per skein]:

☐ 2 skeins

Crochet Hook

☐ Size K (6.5 mm) **or** size needed for gauge

GAUGE INFORMATION

In pattern, 2 repeats = 3¼" (8.25 cm); 4 rows = 2¼" (5.75 cm)

Gauge Swatch: 6" wide x 4" high (15.25 cm x 10 cm)

Ch 16.

Rows 1-7: Work same as Scarf, page14: 12 sc and 3 ch-1 sps.
Finish off.

INSTRUCTIONS
SCARF

Ch 180.

Row 1: Sc in second ch from hook and in next 2 chs, ★ ch 1, skip next ch, sc in next 3 chs; repeat from ★ across: 135 sc and 44 ch-1 sps.

Row 2 (Right side)**:** Ch 4 (**counts as first dc plus ch 1, now and throughout**), turn; skip next 2 sc, 3 dc in next ch-1 sp, ★ ch 1, skip next 3 sc, 3 dc in next ch-1 sp; repeat from ★ across to last 3 sc, ch 1, skip next 2 sc, dc in last sc: 134 dc and 45 ch-1 sps.

Note: Loop a short piece of yarn around any stitch to mark Row 2 as **right** side.

Row 3: Ch 1, turn; sc in first dc, sc in next ch-1 sp and in next dc, ★ ch 1, skip next dc, sc in next dc, sc in next ch-1 sp and in next dc; repeat from ★ across: 135 sc and 44 ch-1 sps.

Row 4: Ch 4, turn; skip next 2 sc, 3 dc in next ch-1 sp, ★ ch 1, skip next 3 sc, 3 dc in next ch-1 sp; repeat from ★ across to last 3 sc, ch 1, skip next 2 sc, dc in last sc: 134 dc and 45 ch-1 sps.

Rows 5-9: Repeat Rows 3 and 4 twice, then repeat Row 3 once **more**: 135 sc and 44 ch-1 sps.

Finish off.

HOOD

Row 1: With **right** side of Scarf facing, skip first 16 ch-1 sps and  join yarn with dc in next sc *(see Joining With Dc, page 31)*; ch 1, skip next 2 sc, 3 dc in next ch-1 sp, ★ ch 1, skip next 3 sc, 3 dc in next ch-1 sp; repeat from ★ 10 times **more**, ch 1, skip next 2 sc, dc in next sc, leave remaining 16 ch-1 sps unworked: 38 dc and 13 ch-1 sps.

Row 2: Ch 1, turn; sc in first dc, sc in next ch-1 sp and in next dc, ★ ch 1, skip next dc, sc in next dc, sc in next ch-1 sp and in next dc; repeat from ★ across: 39 sc and 12 ch-1 sps.

Row 3: Ch 4, turn; skip next 2 sc, 3 dc in next ch-1 sp, ★ ch 1, skip next 3 sc, 3 dc in next ch-1 sp; repeat from ★ across to last 3 sc, ch 1, skip next 2 sc, dc in last sc: 38 dc and 13 ch-1 sps.

Rows 4-6: Repeat Rows 2 and 3 once, then repeat Row 2 once **more**: 39 sc and 12 ch-1 sps.

Joining Row (Back Hood seam)**:** Ch 1, turn;  fold Hood in half with **right** side together; matching sts on Row 6 and working through **outside** loops of **both** thicknesses, sc in each st across; finish off.

EDGING

With **right** side of Scarf facing and  working in free loops of beginning ch *(Fig. 3, page 31)*, join yarn with dc in ch at base of first sc; 2 dc in same st, (ch 1, skip next ch, dc in next 3 chs) across to last 2 chs, ch 1, skip next ch, 3 dc in last ch, ch 1; (3 dc, ch 1) around dc at end of each dc row across;

working across unworked sts on Row 9 of Scarf, 3 dc in first sc, (ch 1, skip next sc, dc in next sc, dc in next ch-1 sp and in next sc) across to last 2 sc, ch 1, skip last 2 sc and last ch-1 sp; (3 dc, ch 1) around dc at end of each dc row across Hood; working across unworked sts on Row 9 of Scarf, ch 1, skip first ch-1 sp and first 2 sc, dc in next sc, dc in next ch-1 sp and in next sc, (ch 1, skip next sc, dc in next sc, dc in next ch-1 sp and in next sc) across to last 2 sc, ch 1, skip next sc, 3 dc in last sc, ch 1; (3 dc, ch 1) around dc at end of each dc row across; join with slip st to first dc, finish off.

Design by Lois J. Long.

LAUREN

 **EASY**

Finished Scarf Measurement:

7" x 69½" (18 cm x 176.5 cm)

Finished Hood Size:

One size fits most Adults

SHOPPING LIST

Yarn (Medium Weight)

[3.5 ounces, 197 yards (100 grams, 180 meters) per skein]:

☐ 3 skeins

Crochet Hook

☐ Size H (5 mm) **or** size needed for gauge

GAUGE INFORMATION

In pattern, 2 repeats (8 sts) = 2½" (6.25 cm); 8 rows = 3¾" (9.5 cm)

Gauge Swatch: 4" x 3¾" (10 cm x 9.5 cm)

Ch 16.

Rows 1-8: Work same as Scarf, page 18: 13 sts.

Finish off.

INSTRUCTIONS
SCARF

Ch 224.

Row 1 (Right side)**:** Dc in fourth ch from hook **(3 skipped chs counts as first dc)**, skip next ch, sc in next ch, ★ skip next ch, 3 dc in next ch, skip next ch, sc in next ch; repeat from ★ across to last 2 chs, skip next ch, 2 dc in last ch: 221 sts.

Note: Loop a short piece of yarn around any stitch to mark Row 1 as **right** side.

Row 2: Ch 1, turn; sc in first dc, skip next dc, 3 dc in next sc, ★ skip next dc, sc in next dc, skip next dc, 3 dc in next sc; repeat from ★ across to last 2 dc, skip next dc, sc in last dc.

Row 3: Ch 3 **(counts as first dc, now and throughout)**, turn; dc in first sc, skip next dc, sc in next dc, ★ skip next dc, 3 dc in next sc, skip next dc, sc in next dc; repeat from ★ across to last 2 sts, skip next dc, 2 dc in last sc.

Row 4: Ch 1, turn; sc in first dc, skip next dc, 3 dc in next sc, ★ skip next dc, sc in next dc, skip next dc, 3 dc in next sc; repeat from ★ across to last 2 dc, skip next dc, sc in last dc.

Row 5: Ch 3, turn; dc in first sc, skip next dc, sc in next dc, ★ skip next dc, 3 dc in next sc, skip next dc, sc in next dc; repeat from ★ across to last 2 sts, skip next dc, 2 dc in last sc.

Rows 6-14: Repeat Rows 4 and 5, 4 times; then repeat Row 4 once **more**: 221 sts.

Finish off.

HOOD

Row 1: With **right** side of Scarf facing, skip first 80 sts and 🎥 join yarn with dc in next sc *(see Joining With Dc, page 31)*; dc in same sc, skip next dc, sc in next dc, ★ skip next dc, 3 dc in next sc, skip next dc, sc in next dc; repeat from ★ 13 times **more**, skip next dc, 2 dc in next sc, leave remaining 80 sts unworked: 61 sts.

Row 2: Ch 1, turn; sc in first dc, skip next dc, 3 dc in next sc, ★ skip next dc, sc in next dc, skip next dc, 3 dc in next sc; repeat from ★ across to last 2 dc, skip next dc, sc in last dc.

Row 3: Ch 3, turn; dc in first sc, skip next dc, sc in next dc, ★ skip next dc, 3 dc in next sc, skip next dc, sc in next dc; repeat from ★ across to last 2 sts, skip next dc, 2 dc in last sc.

Rows 4-9: Repeat Rows 2 and 3, 3 times: 61 sts.

Joining Row (Back Hood seam)**:** Ch 1, turn;  fold Hood in half with **right** side together; matching sts on Row 9 and working through **outside** loops of **both** thicknesses, sc in each st across; finish off.

EDGING

Rnd 1: With **right** side of Scarf facing, join yarn with sc *(see Joining With Sc, page 31)* in free loop of first ch *(Fig. 3, page 31)*; sc evenly around entire piece working 3 sc in each corner; join with slip st to first sc, finish off.

Design by Lois J. Long.

MEGHAN

 **EASY**

Finished Scarf Measurement:

8" x 71½" (20.5 cm x 181.5 cm)

Finished Hood Size:

One size fits most Adults

SHOPPING LIST

Yarn (Medium Weight)

[3.5 ounces, 170 yards (100 grams, 156 meters) per skein]:

☐ 5 skeins

Crochet Hook

☐ Size I (5.5 mm) **or** size needed for gauge

GAUGE INFORMATION

In pattern, 13 sts and 10 rows = 4¼" (10.75 cm)

Gauge Swatch: 4¼" (10.75 cm) square

Ch 14.

Rows 1-10: Work same as Scarf: 13 sts.

Finish off.

——— STITCH GUIDE ———

TREBLE CROCHET *(abbreviated tr)*
YO twice, insert hook in st indicated,
YO and pull up a loop (4 loops on
hook), (YO and draw through 2 loops
on hook) 3 times. Push tr to **right** side
as next stitch is worked.

INSTRUCTIONS
SCARF
Ch 218.

Row 1 (Right side)**:** Sc in second ch
from hook, (tr in next ch, sc in next ch)
across: 217 sts.

Note: Loop a short piece of yarn
around any stitch to mark Row 1 as
right side.

Row 2: Ch 1, turn; sc in first 2 sts, tr
in next sc, (sc in next tr, tr in next sc)
across to last 2 sts, sc in last 2 sts.

Row 3: Ch 1, turn; sc in first sc, (tr in
next sc, sc in next st) across.

Rows 4-18: Repeat Rows 2 and 3,
7 times; then repeat Row 2 once **more**:
217 sts.

Finish off.

HOOD
Row 1: With **right** side of Scarf facing,
skip first 78 sts and join yarn
with sc in next tr *(see Joining With
Sc, page 31)*; (tr in next sc, sc in next
tr) 30 times, leave remaining 78 sts
unworked: 61 sts.

Row 2: Ch 1, turn; sc in first 2 sts, tr
in next sc, (sc in next tr, tr in next sc)
across to last 2 sts, sc in last 2 sts.

Row 3: Ch 1, turn; sc in first sc, (tr in
next sc, sc in next st) across.

Rows 4-10: Repeat Rows 2 and 3,
3 times; then repeat Row 2 once **more**:
61 sts.

Joining Row (Back Hood seam)**:** Ch 1,
turn; fold Hood in half with **right**
side together; matching sts on Row 10
and working through **outside** loops of
both thicknesses, sc in each st across;
finish off.

EDGING
Rnd 1: With **right** side of Scarf facing,
join yarn with sc in free loop of
first ch *(Fig. 3, page 31)*; sc evenly
around entire piece working 3 sc in
each corner; join with slip st to first sc,
finish off.

Design by Lois J. Long.

21

BECKY

 **EASY**

Finished Scarf Measurement:

7¾" x 73¼" (19.5 cm x 186 cm)

Finished Hood Size:

One size fits most Adults

SHOPPING LIST

Yarn (Medium Weight)

[3.5 ounces, 197 yards (100 grams, 180 meters) per skein]:

☐ 4 skeins

Crochet Hook

☐ Size H (5 mm) **or** size needed for gauge

GAUGE INFORMATION

In pattern, 2 repeats (12 sts) = 3¼" (8.25 cm);

   8 rows = 4" (10 cm)

Gauge Swatch: 4½" x 4¼" (11.5 cm x 10.75 cm)

Ch 19.

Rows 1-9: Work same as Scarf, page 24: 17 sts.

Finish off.

——— STITCH GUIDE ———

🎥 FRONT POST DOUBLE CROCHET

(abbreviated FPdc)

YO, insert hook from **front** to **back** around post of st indicated (*Fig. 4, page 31*), YO and pull up a loop (3 loops on hook), (YO and draw through 2 loops on hook) twice.

🎥 BACK POST DOUBLE CROCHET

(abbreviated BPdc)

YO, insert hook from **back** to **front** around post of st indicated (*Fig. 4, page 31*), YO and pull up a loop (3 loops on hook), (YO and draw through 2 loops on hook) twice.

INSTRUCTIONS
SCARF

Ch 271.

Row 1 (Right side)**:** Dc in fourth ch from hook (**3 skipped chs count as first dc**) and in each ch across: 269 dc.

Note: Loop a short piece of yarn around any stitch to mark Row 1 as **right** side.

Row 2: Ch 3 (**counts as first dc, now and throughout**), turn; work FPdc around each of next 3 dc, ★ work BPdc around each of next 3 dc, work FPdc around each of next 3 dc; repeat from ★ across to last dc, dc in last dc.

Rows 3-14: Ch 3, turn; work FPdc around each of next 3 FPdc, ★ work BPdc around each of next 3 BPdc, work FPdc around each of next 3 FPdc; repeat from ★ across to last dc, dc in last dc.

Finish off.

HOOD

Row 1: With **right** side of Scarf facing, skip first 99 sts and  join yarn with dc in next FPdc *(see Joining With Dc, page 31)*; work BPdc around each of next 3 BPdc, ★ work FPdc around each of next 3 FPdc, work BPdc around each of next 3 BPdc; repeat from ★ 10 times **more**, dc in next FPdc, leave remaining 99 sts unworked: 71 sts.

Rows 2-9: Ch 3, turn; work BPdc around each of next 3 BPdc, ★ work FPdc around each of next 3 FPdc, work BPdc around each of next 3 BPdc; repeat from ★ across to last dc, dc in last dc.

Joining Row (Back Hood seam)**:** Ch 1, turn; fold Hood in half with **right** side together; matching sts on Row 9 and working through **outside** loops of **both** thicknesses, sc in each st across; finish off.

EDGING

Rnd 1: With **right** side of Scarf facing, join yarn with sc *(see Joining With Sc, page 31)* in free loop of first ch *(Fig. 3, page 31)*; sc evenly around entire piece working 3 sc in each corner; join with slip st to first sc.

Rnd 2: Ch 1; working from **left** to **right**, work reverse sc in next sc *(Figs. 5a-d, page 31)* and in each sc around; join with slip st to first st, finish off.

Design by Lois J. Long.

CARLA

 **EASY**

Finished Scarf Measurement:

5½" x 71½" (14 cm x 181.5 cm)

Finished Hood Size:

One size fits most Adults

SHOPPING LIST

Yarn (Medium Weight)

[3.5 ounces, 170 yards (100 grams, 156 meters) per skein]:

☐ 3 skeins

Crochet Hook

☐ Size I (5.5 mm) **or** size needed for gauge

GAUGE INFORMATION

In pattern, 2 repeats = 3" (7.5 cm); Rows 1-8 = 4¼" (10.75 cm)

Gauge Swatch: 5¼" x 4¼" (13.25 cm x 10.75 cm)

Ch 16.

Rows 1-8: Work same as Scarf, page 28: 18 sts and 3 ch-1 sps.

Finish off.

STITCH GUIDE

🎥 FRONT POST DOUBLE CROCHET
(abbreviated FPdc)

YO, insert hook from **front** to **back** around post of st indicated *(Fig. 4, page 31)*, YO and pull up a loop (3 loops on hook), (YO and draw through 2 loops on hook) twice.

🎥 BACK POST DOUBLE CROCHET
(abbreviated BPdc)

YO, insert hook from **back** to **front** around post of st indicated *(Fig. 4, page 31)*, YO and pull up a loop (3 loops on hook), (YO and draw through 2 loops on hook) twice.

INSTRUCTIONS
SCARF
Ch 192.

Row 1 (Right side)**:** Sc in second ch from hook and in each ch across: 191 sc.

Note: Loop a short piece of yarn around any stitch to mark Row 1 as **right** side.

Row 2: Ch 3, turn; dc in next sc and in each sc across.

Row 3: Ch 1, turn; sc in first dc, work FPdc around next dc, ★ skip next dc, (2 dc, ch 1, 2 dc) in next dc, skip next dc, work FPdc around next dc; repeat from ★ across to last dc, sc in last dc: 238 sts and 47 ch-1 sps.

Row 4: Ch 1, turn; sc in first sc, work BPdc around next FPdc, ★ skip next 2 dc, (2 dc, ch 1, 2 dc) in next ch-1 sp, skip next 2 dc, work BPdc around next FPdc; repeat from ★ across to last sc, sc in last sc.

Row 5: Ch 1, turn; sc in first sc, work FPdc around next BPdc, ★ skip next 2 dc, (2 dc, ch 1, 2 dc) in next ch-1 sp, skip next 2 dc, work FPdc around next BPdc; repeat from ★ across to last sc, sc in last sc.

Rows 6-8: Repeat Rows 4 and 5 once, then repeat Row 4 once **more**: 238 sts and 47 ch-1 sps.

Finish off.

HOOD

Row 1: With **right** side of Scarf facing, skip first 17 ch-1 sps and next dc,  join yarn with sc in next dc *(see Joining With Sc, page 31)*; work FPdc around next BPdc, ★ skip next 2 dc, (2 dc, ch 1, 2 dc) in next ch-1 sp, skip next 2 dc, work FPdc around next BPdc; repeat from ★ 12 times **more**, sc in next dc, leave remaining 17 ch-1 sps unworked: 68 sts and 13 ch-1 sps.

Row 2: Ch 1, turn; sc in first sc, work BPdc around next FPdc, ★ skip next 2 dc, (2 dc, ch 1, 2 dc) in next ch-1 sp, skip next 2 dc, work BPdc around next FPdc; repeat from ★ across to last sc, sc in last sc.

Row 3: Ch 1, turn; sc in first sc, work FPdc around next BPdc, ★ skip next 2 dc, (2 dc, ch 1, 2 dc) in next ch-1 sp, skip next 2 dc, work FPdc around next BPdc; repeat from ★ across to last sc, sc in last sc.

Rows 4-9: Repeat Rows 2 and 3, 3 times: 68 sts and 13 ch-1 sps.

Joining Row (Back Hood seam)**:** Ch 1, turn; fold Hood in half with **right** side together; matching sts on Row 9 and working through **outside** loops of **both** thicknesses, sc in each st across; finish off.

EDGING

With **right** side of Scarf facing, and working in free loops of beginning ch *(Fig. 3, page 31)*; join yarn with sc in first ch; 2 sc in same ch, sc in next ch, ★ skip next ch, (2 dc, ch 1, 2 dc) in next ch, skip next ch, sc in next ch; repeat from ★ across to ch at base of first sc, 3 sc in next ch; sc evenly around remainder of piece working 3 sc in each corner; join with slip st to first sc, finish off.

Design by Lois J. Long.

GENERAL INSTRUCTIONS

ABBREVIATIONS

BPdc	Back Post double crochet(s)
ch(s)	chain(s)
cm	centimeters
dc	double crochet(s)
FPdc	Front Post double crochet(s)
FPsc	Front Post single crochet(s)
mm	millimeters
Rnd(s)	Round(s)
sc	single crochet(s)
sp(s)	space(s)
st(s)	stitch(es)
tr	treble crochet(s)
YO	yarn over

SYMBOLS & TERMS

★ — work instructions following ★ as many **more** times as indicated in addition to the first time.

( ) or [ ] — work enclosed instructions **as many** times as specified by the number immediately following **or** work all enclosed instructions in the stitch or space indicated **or** contains explanatory remarks.

colon (:) — the number(s) given after a colon at the end of a row or round denote(s) the number of stitches or spaces you should have on that row or round.

Yarn Weight Symbol & Names	LACE 0	SUPER FINE 1	FINE 2	LIGHT 3	MEDIUM 4	BULKY 5	SUPER BULKY 6
Type of Yarns in Category	Fingering, 10-count crochet thread	Sock, Fingering Baby	Sport, Baby	DK, Light Worsted	Worsted, Afghan, Aran	Chunky, Craft, Rug	Bulky, Roving
Crochet Gauge* Ranges in Single Crochet to 4" (10 cm)	32-42 double crochets**	21-32 sts	16-20 sts	12-17 sts	11-14 sts	8-11 sts	5-9 sts
Advised Hook Size Range	Steel*** 6,7,8 Regular hook B-1	B-1 to E-4	E-4 to 7	7 to I-9	I-9 to K-10.5	K-10.5 to M-13	M-13 and larger

*GUIDELINES ONLY: The chart above reflects the most commonly used gauges and hook sizes for specific yarn categories.

** Lace weight yarns are usually crocheted on larger-size hooks to create lacy openwork patterns. Accordingly, a gauge range is difficult to determine. Always follow the gauge stated in your pattern.

*** Steel crochet hooks are sized differently from regular hooks–the higher the number the smaller the hook, which is the reverse of regular hook sizing.

CROCHET TERMINOLOGY	
UNITED STATES	**INTERNATIONAL**
slip stitch (slip st)	= single crochet (sc)
single crochet (sc)	= double crochet (dc)
half double crochet (hdc)	= half treble crochet (htr)
double crochet (dc)	= treble crochet(tr)
treble crochet (tr)	= double treble crochet (dtr)
double treble crochet (dtr)	= triple treble crochet (ttr)
triple treble crochet (tr tr)	= quadruple treble crochet (qtr)
skip	= miss

CROCHET HOOKS															
U.S.	B-1	C-2	D-3	E-4	F-5	G-6	H-8	I-9	J-10	K-10½	L-11	M/N-13	N/P-15	P/Q	Q	S
Metric - mm	2.25	2.75	3.25	3.5	3.75	4	5	5.5	6	6.5	8	9	10	15	16	19

■□□□ **BEGINNER**	Projects for first-time crocheters using basic stitches. Minimal shaping.
■■□□ **EASY**	Projects using yarn with basic stitches, repetitive stitch patterns, simple color changes, and simple shaping and finishing.
■■■□ **INTERMEDIATE**	Projects using a variety of techniques, such as basic lace patterns or color patterns, mid-level shaping and finishing.
■■■■ **EXPERIENCED**	Projects with intricate stitch patterns, techniques and dimension, such as non-repeating patterns, multi-color techniques, fine threads, small hooks, detailed shaping and refined finishing.

GAUGE

Exact gauge is essential for proper size. Before beginning your project, make the sample swatch given in the individual instructions in the yarn and hook specified. After completing the swatch, measure it, counting your stitches and rows carefully. If your swatch is larger or smaller than specified **make another, changing hook size to get the correct gauge**. Keep trying until you find the size hook that will give you the specified gauge.

JOINING WITH SC

When instructed to join with sc, begin with a slip knot on the hook. Insert the hook in the stitch or space indicated, YO and pull up a loop, YO and draw through both loops on hook.

JOINING WITH DC

When instructed to join with dc, begin with a slip knot on the hook. YO, holding loop on hook, insert the hook in the stitch or space indicated, YO and pull up a loop (3 loops on hook), (YO and draw through 2 loops on hook) twice.

FREE LOOPS

When instructed to work in free loops of a chain, work in loop indicated by arrow *(Fig. 3)*.

Fig. 3

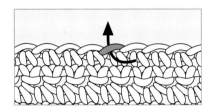

POST STITCH

Work around the post of the stitch indicated, inserting the hook in the direction of the arrow *(Fig. 4)*.

Fig. 4

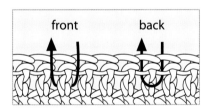

REVERSE SINGLE CROCHET

(abbreviated reverse sc)

Working from left to **right**, ★ insert hook in st to right of hook *(Fig. 5a)*, YO and draw through, under and to left of loop on hook (2 loops on hook) *(Fig. 5b)*, YO and draw through both loops on hook *(Fig. 5c)* (reverse sc made, *Fig. 5d)*; repeat from ★ around.

Fig. 5a

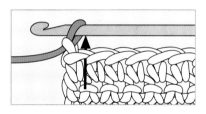

Fig. 5b

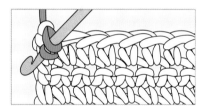

Fig. 5c

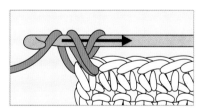

Fig. 5d

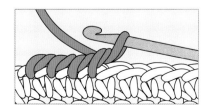

YARN INFORMATION

The Hooded Scarves in this book were made using Medium Weight or Bulky Weight Yarn. Any brand of Medium Weight or Bulky Weight Yarn may be used. It is best to refer to the yardage/meters when determining how many balls or skeins to purchase. Remember, to arrive at the finished size, it is the GAUGE/TENSION that is important, not the brand of yarn.

For your convenience, listed below are the specific yarns used to create our photography models.

EMMA
Red Heart® With Love®
Berry - #1907 Boysenberry
Grey - #1401 Pewter

LISA
Caron® Simply Soft®
#9756 Lavender Blue

CHERIE
Red Heart® With Love®
#1914 Berry Red

ANGELINA
Lion Brand® Homespun®
#396 Fiesta

LAUREN
Bernat® Waverly
#55280 Celadon

MEGHAN
Lion Brand® Vanna's Choice®
#124 Toffee

BECKY
Bernat® Waverly
#55008 Birch White

CARLA
Lion Brand® Vanna's Choice®
#107 Sapphire

We have made every effort to ensure that these instructions are accurate and complete. We cannot, however, be responsible for human error, typographical mistakes, or variations in individual work.

Production Team: Instructional/Technical Editor - Lois J. Long; Editorial Writer - Susan Frantz Wiles; Senior Graphic Artist - Lora Puls; Graphic Artist - Becca Snider Tally; Photo Stylist - Brooke Duszota; and Photographer - Jason Masters.

Instructions tested and photos models made by Janet Akins and Marianna Crowder.